OUTTAKES

OUTTAKES

JOANNA ACEVEDO

Edited by Peg Alford Pursell
Designed by Diamond Braxton
Cover photograph by lil artsy

Library of Congress Cataloging-in-Publication data is on file with the Library of Congress.
Acevedo, Joanna.
Outtakes / Joanna Acevedo
ISBN 978-1-7336619-7-3 (pbk) | 978-1-7336619-8-0 (ebook)

Published by WTAW Press
PO Box 2825
Santa Rosa, CA 95405
www.wtawpress.org

WTAW Press is a not-for-profit literary press. We are grateful for the assistance we receive from individual donors, public arts agencies, and private foundations.

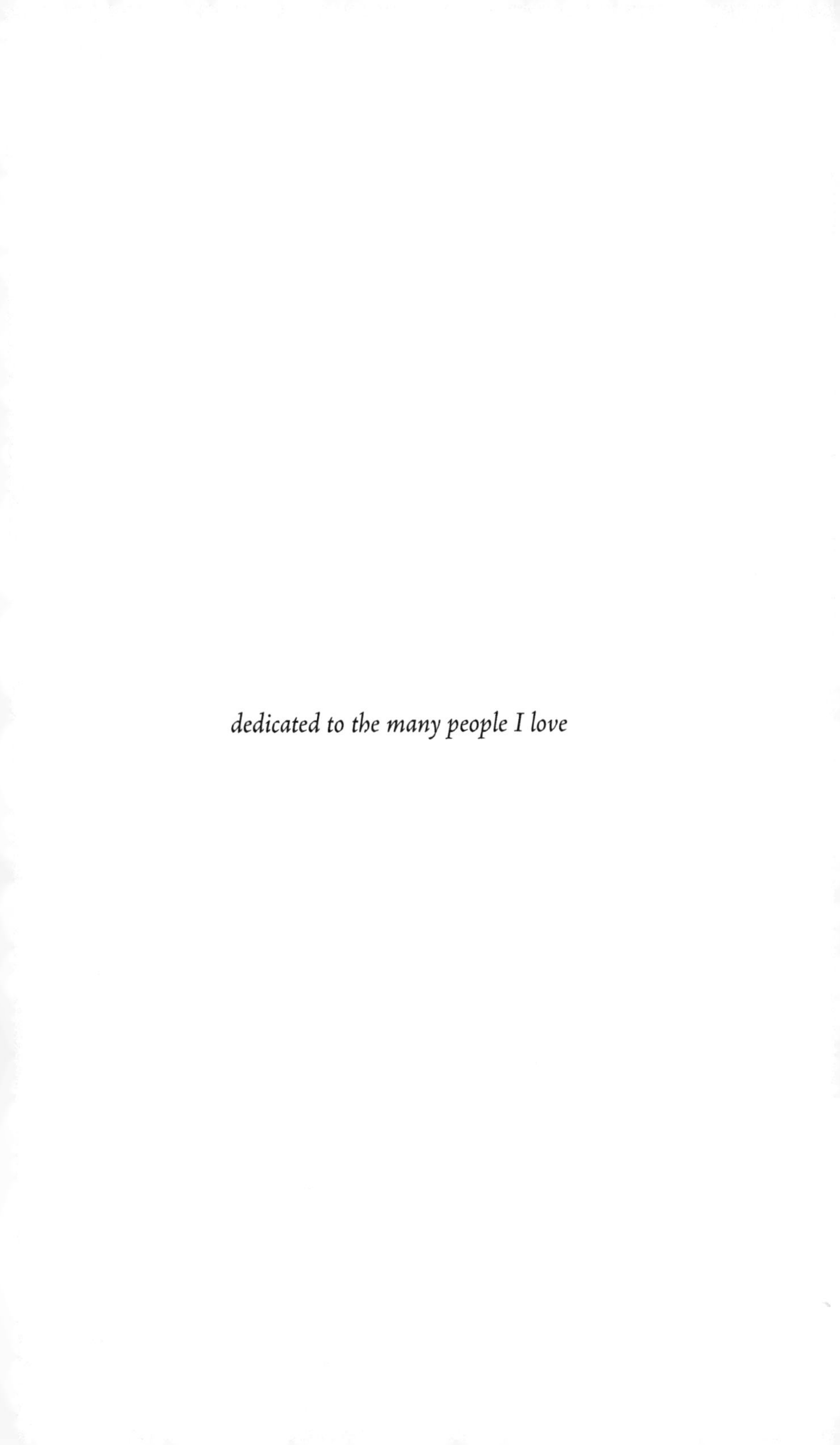

dedicated to the many people I love

Contents

How Joyous We Once Were

In September, a squirrel drops from the heavens to land on my air conditioner and scare the shit out of us as we talk about our conflicting diagnoses. I've long ago stopped taking my lithium. We're spinning in each other's orbits. It happens before it happens. I'm a horse with a bit in my mouth.

Watching her do the dishes. I like the way she moves around the kitchen: purposeful, every movement sure. She tells me about her long short stories, the personal essay about plums. I'm busy worrying about nuclear holocaust. Imagining being someone's wife. She made too much food, while I showed up late, and tripping on acid. I pick at the cheese plate, eat an entire wheel of brie, stand in her kitchen listening to the cadence of her voice. The floor wavers.

I am queen of the rodents. On our walk, we see a skunk hissing near a garbage can, keep walking. Astoria in the middle of the night is quiet, residential, provincial. I wonder aloud who's driving at this time of night; it's three or four in the morning. "People have places to go," she says.

I want to be her hands on the plates in the sink, warm with soapy water. I want to be the dishwasher humming, the heat from the oven making the whole kitchen steamy. In this bright box of a kitchen, we are two still points of light, two converging dots on a scoreboard. What's the score? No one knows.

We're constantly talking in what-ifs, the future tense present in our verbs and ad-verbiage. The book we want to write exists in our minds, the exchange of ideas fluid and easy. "What if we just transcribed these conversations?" she says. "I think that would be a lot less interesting than we think it is," I tell her.

In the morning, we eat spinach pie and drink cider. The kitchen is full of light. I am a part of a whole, a connection in a web of larger webs. I'm trying to find myself in a set of commands. Looking for where I fit in the grand scheme. I suspect she is doing the same.

In my dream, I thought she woke me up from sleep. I thought she said, "Good morning, it's time to get up." When I awoke, she was gone from the room, and there was only an open window.

Someone Wants to Be Your Friend

Lately I've been sleeping so deeply that I've been forgetting where I am, that I'm even a human being. The dreamworld is so compelling, so all-consuming. When I wake up, I'm surprised to be *just* me, present-day, lying sweaty and tangled in the bedsheets.

Recently, I've had a hard time remembering people's names, faces. It all smears together into one flesh-colored blur, and I have a difficult time picking out who is important and who is simply background noise. I also have a hard time picking out the literal background noise. Everything is humming, and I can't tell the important conversation from the drone of the car alarms outside in the street.

Your phone can remind you to call your mother, drink water, make doctor's appointments, but it can't remind you to be a better person. It can't remind you to be a good friend, a conscientious voter, a port in the storm. We put our trust in these systems, but what happens when these systems put their trust in *us?*

I get a Snapchat alert: "Someone wants to be your friend!"

Maybe the problem is I'm a narcissist. I've always believed writing involves a certain level of narcissism, at least personal writing, given the level of self-obsession needed to do the self-reflection integral to the process. At a talk I attended at NYU early in my graduate-level education, Etgar Keret commented that being a writer doesn't imply having more knowledge than the general population. Actually, it means that one knows *less* than most people, because a writer is voluntarily choosing to sit in a dark room and think about the human condition for hours at a time. "I have *less* answers than you do!" he crowed, a small man with gray hair, gleeful in his ignorance. I laughed along with the rest of the room, but the prospect disturbed me.

"Don't let anyone tell you your poetry is too confessional," someone told me at a poetry reading recently. "You're working in a tradition: Sylvia, Anne, Robert." No one had ever told me my poetry was too confessional. This woman was drunk, and I wondered if she was indirectly telling me just that, but I smiled and showed her the Anne Sexton line tattooed on my chest. I had just read a poem aloud at a well-attended reading about my summer suicide attempt. I felt like I was wearing a big sign on my head that said: CRAZY. It's amazing what you can share with strangers, what so-called civilized people will tolerate.

At a different reading, I watched a woman pull her own manifesto out of her vagina to read it. At least I'm not doing that,

I thought. People congratulated this woman on how provocative and thought-provoking her performance was. I left the room, called my mother, and said, "I could have done without that."

People continuously confess their secrets to me. I've always had a satellite dish quality, a kind of open bookishness that makes people want to tell me things. It all goes into the writing, like it's been directly funneled into a meat grinder, a kind of karmic vomit I can neither control nor explain. Family dramas, relationship woes, cancer diagnoses: it all gets swirled together, running down into the toilet bowl of my creative enterprise.

I'm constantly looking for lucky charms, good omens. I'm superstitious. I try not to step on the cracks in the sidewalk. I don't walk under ladders. I knock on wood. The world is so random and surprising, I want some kind of order, some way to govern the way it works. This is an illusion. There is no way to create order. But as Anne Carson once told me, "A blessing is just another way of looking at a curse."

"What if I just kept reading, and never stopped?" joked my friend Rob at a literary event. It played into all our deepest fears as literary citizens. His poems are beautiful, but all of us were worried. Without some contrast—beauty and ugliness, the ambient noise of the city around us, the grinding of someone's buzzsaw in a nearby backyard—his poems would have less weight. There needed to be a beginning and an end. We needed to be able to bracket his reading within our own lives to understand that sometimes good things finish and new things begin.

Recently at the McNally Jackson bookstore, a presenter claimed she was a lesbian who primarily dated men. Laughter floated up to the ceiling. I love a good contradiction—it keeps me on my toes. People are primarily made up of these juxtapositions, this cognitive dissonance. How much you make sense to yourself is dependent on how much you can bore through the noise.

I get a Co-Star alert: "Share your poetry with others."

I'm always looking for answers. How to write, how to live. I'm looking through the window of a taxicab on Flushing Avenue: the world passes me by in a slurry of neon. I've heard that the moon holds all the answers in her mouth. I can see them if I squint my eyes after too many cups of liquid gold.

Once I told you I would write something that wasn't about you. I'm still working on it.

Color Theory

He complains that I don't smile in photographs, so I send him smiling selfies from miles away, bridging the proximate gap between our two bodies with my mouth upturned like half a grape. "Belle," he says, his high school French just good enough to confuse me. Separately, we rot our teeth with soda and consume massive amounts of black tea. He's an extension of my body, a phantom limb I can neither remove nor understand. If I were a color, I would be scarlet red.

In the KGB Red Room on a Monday night, I achieve the perfect level of drunk and high on tequila and cocaine and feel my body humming like a wire. I could live forever in this moment, watching people switch in and off the open mic, embarrassingly baring their creative souls in front of a crowd of disinterested strangers. Guitar and piano twangs. I read, my voice tripping over the syllables. After, we get pizza I don't eat, conversations flowing like wine. Everything feels meaningful, and nothing is.

Who said I can't do this better? Who says I can't live forever?

We're all looking for that perfect moment, that second when we reach equilibrium. Crushed into his chest in Nashville, I was there. Flash forward: he's leaving, his shoulder bag over his shoulder, the cat escaping, me falling to my knees on the landing in tears. We make up over the phone a week later, but I'm already gone, already in Minnesota before I head back to New York, the distance like a yawning mouth swallowing me up before I can grab a foothold.

If I were a color, I would be cerulean blue.

At the bar, also on a Monday night, I kiss everyone on the cheek and stifle my yawns. The drugs are gone. There are only my feet in sandals, my Bud Lite T-shirt. Pool balls cracking, drinks clinking in heavy-bottomed glasses. We're all reaching like baby birds with open mouths for someone to feed us more alcohol, more love, more of anything. The Uber comes and we get in, tripping onto the leather seats and reclining with our eyes out of focus so the neon of the city looks like a 7-Eleven Slushie of light.

He tells me to "Be safe," his voice hesitant over text. I can feel his fear like a living thing. Our bodies separated by miles and miles, he cannot scoop me up like I know he wants to and protect me from the world's disruptions. I know this feeling because I feel it too. I tap out bumps from the vial in the bathroom and text him pictures of myself smiling on the train, in the bar, on the street, so he knows I'm alright, I'm happy, I'm having a good time without him. I don't know if this is good or bad. I don't know anything at all.

All I want is to be loved, unconditionally, by everyone I meet. I say "I love you" loosely, listen for the flat automatic way he slurs it back, whiskey on his breath. I crave approval the way a dog craves a bone, his hand on my thigh in the Uber, his lips on my neck, my collarbone. I'm not desperate but I could be desperate.

If I were a color, I would be canary yellow.

Separate Houses

1.

I don't know how to be—I never know where to put my hands, for example. Social niceties elude me. Ask me how I'm doing: you'll get a monologue, an overshare, a diatribe. I'm confused. I'm confusing. Being a person is like a class I never took, or attended but failed, the teacher shaking their head and telling me to repeat the seminar.

Normally, I can hide my impossibility. I'm very good at smiling, nodding, and pretending I know what you just said. But once in a while, I slip. The house of cards teeters, then falls to the floor. Feathers everywhere. The soup on the stove is burning, and I've locked myself out of the house.

—

In the mornings, I paint on my face. The lipstick, the eyeliner.

I have been drawing a new face on top of my real one for as long as I have been an adult, and even before that. It's been so long I'm not sure what I really look like anymore. I'm not sure which face is the real me.

It's like armor—a barrier between me and the real world. Upheavals in recent memory: black eyeliner and a tank top in the eighth grade, men beginning to stare at me on the street. Is this power? This new-found excitement at the thrill of someone else's body in conjunction with my own?

In the words of Chen Chen: "To realize some of my writing is just my saying to white men: Look how lovable I am."

—

And now the realization: I was a child. At thirteen, roaming the city with a cellphone and a cigarette. It's no wonder I'm poorly equipped for the machinations of adulthood. Bless my parents, they did the best they could. I was too ready to be wild, too ready to be reckless.

A story about the body: a bowl full of dead bees.

2.

I try to do this all the time: condense my own history into a series of gestures, but there is no way to do it. According to quantum mechanics, you are not a person, you are a series of events. Speech, as my father tells me one day over Thai food in a cramped restaurant on Seventh Avenue, is a useless medium. That's why he's uninterested in talking about his feelings. My gentle father, who has basically no friends, is uninterested in the basic mode of human communication. I admire him.

I turn to marks on paper, keystrokes on a computer, as a way to record what has happened to me. Not because my historical record is so important, but because it is mine. Because it is what I know. I write because sometimes, there is nothing to say out loud. Just words written down, twisted and manipulated, handled roughly, and given like a gift you cannot return or exchange. Because I cannot turn it off, I cannot stop. And even if I could, why would I? I have no other way to communicate.

I've always wondered—how do you create a concise history from the body, which is so experiential? The magic of touch, the freneticism of mania, the leaden feeling of depression? A chipped tooth, your lover's fingertips on your back, anxiety pooling in the base of your spine? It almost seems impossible. But we try all the time, hundreds of writers tapping away at keyboards, cigarettes in our mouths, heads in our hands, inches away from giving it up for good.

—

And so the doorbell blips, indicating a package has arrived for me. Despite all indications otherwise, I am a real person. I can be touched, held, taken. Manipulated and moved. The body as a work of fiction. The body as a choice. The body gives and it takes away. That power, yours in relation to someone else's? It's fleeting, like the movement of clouds over the sun.

3.

And so they take and take away from your body. Then you meet the right one, the nice one, who takes just the right way and in the right proportions, and you hold onto them tightly, you never let go. It's impossible to know, will this end properly? With the white dress and the promises? I've been told not to, but I imagine the end—the headstones nestled together in the grove of mango trees. I make promises I can't keep.

I don't know how to love—this is too much, where can I put it down? I feel like I skipped the class on how to be a partner, a friend. I partake in too much joy at others' misery. I don't know how to let myself simply be a person, in the slipstream of conversation, not comparing myself. I've been told again and again: Not everything is a competition.

But it is.

We both sleep in separate houses. A separate roof over his head, a separate roof over mine. I try to bridge the gap with kisses, promises to be better, "I can change."

I can't change. I'm bad at love. I give you all of myself, or I give you nothing.

A story about the body: a bowl full of dead fish.

4.

How to be? "Cogito ergo sum: I think, therefore I am." But how to translate? Like my father, I am having trouble fiddling the dials, making the universe line up just right. Quantum mechanics—the idea that anything, technically, is possible. So why do I feel so limited by choice?

5.

It all comes back to the body—where to put my hands? I want to put them on you, dear. You text me late at night, tell me you've had a long day. "How's the sex, drugs, and rock n' roll?" you ask. I have gone to bed early, after working until my eyes fog over. Taken a sleeping pill.

I had gone to Niagara Falls earlier in the day, watched the water fall over the rocks, rushing and crashing. I was overcome by a feeling of limitlessness, a human smallness at the way things erode and still stay strong. The power of water to heal.

A sunbeam slides over my computer. I know where to put my hands now.

I know how to talk to the world, in my small, human way.

Rules of the Road

Somewhere on the Ohio Turnpike, I learn how to drive on the freeway. Road rage. Chris in the front seat, bandanna and Ray-Bans on, teaching me about the passing lane and the cruising lane. His inimitable 1991 Honda station wagon.

In Michigan, off Dixie Highway, the little house holds friends, joints to smoke, a litany of guns, a bow and arrow for killing deer. My heart like a stick in the mud.

I hear the dog's nails on the floor before I hear the dog. The silence of rural towns. Chickadees and mourning doves at the birdfeeder; one macho black squirrel that rules over all the rest. Pico, the cat, who longs to be outside. My wet hair in the morning freezes to my cheeks even though it's only October. In the garage, Eric tells a story about a possum trapped in a couch. We giggle like high schoolers.

I dose myself with weed, Klonopin, anything to help me sleep in this strange place where there are no ambulances rushing past in the middle of the night, no drunken bar fights, no emergencies.

Here, there are no emergencies.

I am more myself on these long roads that lead to nowhere, stripped down from the city's posturing on the sidewalk and strutting in the bar. I feel less of the self-consciousness that has plagued me throughout my life, throughout all of our lives. Why do we feel so convinced that we need to care what other people think? Sometimes there is just this: a deer, a bow and arrow, a hunter's finger pulling back the taut string, waiting for the perfect moment, then letting go.

Michigan Travel Diary

We cross state lines with a bump, and then we're in Michigan. I chew Skittles, drink Sprite. Wish I hadn't quit smoking. The Midwest is flatlands, laughter at Fangboner Road, cornfields as far as the eye can see. Neither of us is allowed in Canada.

One of the Great Lakes, choppy from wind, appears on my right. Chris points out Lake Erie, tells me a story about a freighter that disappeared into its depths. To pass the time, we talk about everything—being a child, his mother kicking him out of the house, my parents and their high expectations, his laundry list of ex-girlfriends. I melt into the passenger seat.

This is living, ostensibly. Crisscrossing the US with as little as possible, gas stations and diner food. In the car, we talk about unalienable rights, passionate voices intertwining over the sound of Sloppy Jane on the stereo, and I get so angry my hands ball into tight white knots. It's impossible to argue with Chris. He's read everything, and he knows more than I do about politics, philosophy, and culture. But I hold my ground. I refuse to give in until we compromise on terminology, semantics. In this way, I keep my dignity. I keep my rights.

I am supposed to be working, supposed to be keeping up with email, but instead I become one with the road as we drive around Michigan, living like animals, eating grilled cheese and drinking soda, making pit stops to smoke weed with Chris' friend Eric in the garage. I can feel myself changing, bit by iron bit.

How close can you be to another person? I used to think I knew. After twelve hours in a car with Chris, not even touching, I feel as close as anyone. I know stories about him that I would never repeat, not even to you. I know the smell of his sweat, the way his hands look on a steering wheel, the way his anxiety manifests.

I think another person is too much to know, in one lifetime. I think it's just too much, and we should all stop trying.

I Wait for His Violence

1.

I can't tolerate being alone but don't want to be with other people. Alone around people, that's how I like it. I love comfortable silences, sitting in the car with his hand on my thigh, the windows down, trying not to get smoke in the cab. We don't have to talk if we don't want to.

On another drive, with someone else, I watch the flare of a cigarette illuminate his face as he races down Flatbush Avenue. I wait for his violence, which I know will come. I watch the light of the dab torch and drink whiskey on ice. *I wait for his violence.*

So much of my life has been waiting for someone to hurt me, and then being surprised when he does.

2.

Someone else doesn't stop when I tell him to stop, leaves beer bottles all over the floor of my apartment on Meeker Avenue, above the BQE. You can always hear it, the highway. It rushes like blood in the ears. He beats me in chess, which is almost more painful. He beats me twice.

Later, when I ask him to leave, he does, but complains about it. I feel sick. He texts me afterwards. I reply, I don't know why.

I don't know why I reply.

3.

I think sometimes that I am always waiting for the other shoe to drop, for him to be terrible. I am always waiting for the Indian sunburn grip around my wrist. I am always waiting. He surprises me every day with a new kind of kindness. That is not to say that he does not know how to be cruel, because he does, and often is. But he has never—

4.

Waiting like a loose tooth. Like an appendix you no longer need that swells inside you all the same, causing pain. I can react like a prey animal because I am one. I am the rabbit and the rabbit is me; we run from the wolves.

He buys me a whiskey shot even when I don't want him to. Does it himself. His eyes blurring, his voice turning scarlet. Our hands bathed in red light. "You're mine." "I know." A thousand conversations made up of hand gestures in a bar on Broadway where two people meet and don't have to say anything at all.

5.

Someone else tells me about his wife with a laugh after we've already been involved for two months, leaves Magnums in my trash can, almost rolls off my twin bed in Crown Heights, walks home in the dark.

I lie in the darkness, wondering what just happened. Feeling empty, then full.

We make a joke about it among my friends, but secretly I want to know. I look for him all over the city, follow his footprints, pass his apartment a hundred times in a hundred different Ubers. I never get the courage to knock on the door.

6.

They come and go, and I become a body, a thing. A possession, not a person. He, at eighteen—reckless, high on amphetamines—admits the magnetism between us. I try to kill it with Budweiser down cold throats, cigarettes coughed up like hairballs, acid tabs melting on my tongue.

He, at twenty-four—the most important person in my life, the keeper of my secrets.

I wait for his violence.

7.

I can't count on one hand the ones I've kissed in the taxicabs, outside of bars, on the steps outside of the four different apartment buildings I've lived in. I don't want to count. I can't count the number of times I've stopped myself from being angry.

So much of life is biting your tongue, swallowing your fear, biting the lime wedge that comes with the tequila.

I want to shed my skin.

There he is: lighting the cigarette with his back toward me, walking away.

8.

I don't feel lucky.

The doctors say I am. They have their pills, their diagnoses, their words. They conference call with each other, talk about me behind my back.
Luck is a flavor on the tongue, a penny shoved in a back pocket, a lover who leaves too soon. I'm lucky to have you, I say.

He runs a hand through his hair, unable to take the compliment.

9.

I wait for his violence.

So far, it hasn't come. They all have it in them, I know. They all have that fire in their belly. That curdling in their soul.

But he calls me to tell me, in a slur, that he loves me. When he's scared. When he has seizures. When the moon rises over the house and he needs me there, our bodies approximate, the telepathic connection winking awake.

I don't pick up the phone, I'm asleep, I don't have cell service in this part of Michigan.

We text in the morning. He tells me everything is okay.

And it will be.

10.

Somewhere along the way, I stopped waiting.

The Liminal Space

I believe it when the deli man tells me I'm beautiful, but I can't fathom when my partner tells me "You're not fat" before we have sex.

"Tell me something," he says.

I'm pathologically afraid of distance, want to close the space between our two bodies like you would shut a door. Want to merge our souls. I'm not obsessed, but what I really am is obsessed. Running my hand through the water in the sink like somehow it'll cleanse me.

In our class sessions, Joyce would often mention that I was an obsessive person. Reading my writing, she marked up my drafts to point out my obsessions. Blood, memory. Hungry ghosts.

Interviewing Gaia for the magazine I am working for, I say, "You're like me at eighteen, before alcohol and drugs ruined my brain." Instantly, I feel like a cliche. I am twenty-five, no longer a prodigy, not quite mid-career. I am in the liminal space.

It's a curious thing, to watch someone make the same mistakes you have made. So sure, she steps off the ledge. So confident there will be a net to catch her when she falls. Discussing our first books with Elisa, we laugh about our younger selves. "Don't go in there!" we shout at our previous selves. "Don't follow that man!" But our prior versions don't know what we know now, and they follow those men into the dark.

I love my partner, but sometimes I think we're speaking different languages. He texts me late at night about statistical probability, while I send emails about the interviews I am transcribing. Those hungry ghosts I have never totally managed to shake are cropping up in strange places. Isn't that what love is—finding a common ground in the disparate, making connections in the dusk?

I remember one graduate writing workshop, when Joyce told me to kill off the romantic lead in my story or novel or whatever it was, who was based on the boy I was in love with at the time. "Why doesn't she just kill him?" she asked, her head tremulous like a bird, eighty-three years old. I laughed at the prospect; now it seems obvious. We have to kill our obsessions, before they kill us. We have to set ourselves free.

Love Poem in Eight Parts

1.

We argue about the definition of "normal" over the phone, on a Saturday night, you hours away in another state. It's all about the countdown now: two kids, a Subaru, a house in the suburbs—everything we don't want. You say I've already made a fatal mistake in loving you, if normalcy is what I'm looking for. I almost put down the phone. I'm after Sunday morning movies, cuddling on the couch. "I just want to spend time together," I say. "We will," you promise, your voice high and nasal over the static on the phone line. I wonder when you and I became a we, when we became a unit inseparable from itself.

2.

You argue that I'm probably a better person than you are, ontologically. "You're wonderful," I say, my eyes cloudy with love. Are we in a relationship simply because we're making each other better people? Is that why people couple up, to improve themselves? "See," you say, and I can hear the whiskey rubbing itself into your voice, "That disturbs me. That's Social Darwinism." I exhale, trying to explain my heart with my mouth. "Why can't we just be two people in love?" I ask. "Why does everything have to be a thing?"

3.

We discuss the ways we've changed each other. How you've made me a less dialectical thinker. How I've made you more empathetic. Darwinism or not, we're changing, two drops of water merging and spilling out of my mouth and down my chin.

4.

"Why do you love me?" I ask the ever-present question. "If you think I'm so obsessive and crazy and annoying? If you have all of this anxiety about our relationship?" You drop your phone, trying to smoke weed while talking at the same time, stop and start your answer several times. "Come on," I say. "Just say it."

5.

"Because you understand what I'm saying," you say. "You understand all this shit. Nobody has ever understood what the hell I'm saying before."

6.

All I've ever wanted. To be understood.

7.

Why can't we just be two people in love? I've often wondered. Why do we have to be these fraught creatures, arguing over the phone about the nature of good and evil, past midnight, whiskey churning in our veins? Perhaps it's the whiskey itself that is the culprit. Perhaps it's something within ourselves that forces us to question, to probe, to ask when there is nothing to ask. Simply a shot in the dark.

8.

I don't know the future, but I'm glad I'm not alone in the dark.

Notes

Separate Houses:

The Chen Chen quote comes from his poem, "Summer," in the collection *Your Emergency Contact Has Just Experienced An Emergency*.

The reference to "A story about the body," is from Robert Haas's poem "A Story About the Body."

Acknowledgments

Thank you to these journals, where a few of these essays have previously appeared, sometimes in different forms:

"Rules of the Road," in *Sinking City* (as a poem)

"Someone Wants to Be Your Friend!" in *Chautauqua*

Thank you to the following people: my parents James Acevedo and Anne Finkelstein, Brady Flanigan, Charis Caputo, Anna Kampfe, Nora Goodbody (the ultimate first reader), C. Wednesday (road trip besties for life), Sharon Mesmer, and whoever I've forgotten—there's always someone. Thank you to my agent, Lane Clarke, for all the support, and thank you to Peg Alford Pursell, for seeing something in this weird little book and making it a reality.

Joanna Acevedo is a writer, editor, and educator from New York City. She is the author of two books and two chapbooks, and her writing has been seen across the web and in print, including in *Jelly Bucket*, *Hobart*, and *The Adroit Journal*, among others. She received her MFA in Fiction from New York University in 2021, and also holds degrees from Bard College and The New School.

About WTAW Press

WTAW PRESS IS A 501(C)(3) nonprofit publisher devoted to discovering and publishing enduring literary works of prose. WTAW publishes and champions a carefully curated list of titles across a range of genres (literary fiction, creative nonfiction, and prose that falls somewhere in between), subject matter, and perspectives. WTAW welcomes submissions from writers of all backgrounds and aims to support authors throughout their careers.

As a nonprofit literary press, WTAW depends on the support of donors. We are grateful for the assistance we receive from organizations, foundations, and individuals. WTAW Press especially wishes to thank the following individuals for their sustained support.

Nancy Allen, Lauren Alwan, Robert Ayers, Andrea Barrett, Mary Bonina, Vanessa Bramlett, Harriet Chessman, Melissa Cistaro, Mari Coates, Kathleen Collison, Martha Conway, Michael Croft, Janet S. Crossen, R. Cathay Daniels, Ed Davis, Walt Doll, DB Finnegan, Joan Frank, Helen Fremont, Nancy Garruba, Michelle Georga, Ellen Geohegan, Anne Germanacos and the Germanacos Foundation, Rebecca Godwin, Stephanie Graham, Catherine Grossman, Teresa Burns Gunther, Annie Guthrie, Katie Hafner, Christine Hale, Jo Haraf, Adrianne Harun, Lillian Howan, Yang Huang, Joanna Kalbus, Caroline Kim-Brown, Scott Landers, Ksenija Lakovic, Evan Lavender-Smith, Jeffrey Leong, The Litt Family Foundation, Margot Livesey, Karen Llagas, Nancy Ludmerer, Kevin McIlvoy, Jean Mansen, Sebastian Matthews, Grace Dane Mazur, Kate Milliken, Barbara Moss, Scott Nadelson,

Betty Joyce Nash, Miriam Ormae-Jarmer, Cynthia Phoel, John Philipp, Lee Prusik, Gail Reitano, Joan Silber, Charles Smith, Michael C. Smith, Marian Szczepanski, Kendra Tanacea, Karen Terrey, Renee Thompson, Pete Turchi, Genanne Walsh, Judy Walz, Tracy Winn, Rebecca Winterer, Heather Young, Rolf Yngve, Olga Zilberbourg

To find out more about our mission and publishing program, or to make a donation, please visit wtawpress.org.

WTAW Press provides discounts and auxiliary materials and services for readers. Ebooks are available for purchase at our website book shop. Readers' guides are available for free download from our website. We offer special discounts for all orders of 5 or more books of one title.

Instructors may request examination copies of books they wish to consider for classroom use. If a school's bookstore has already placed an order for a title, a free desk copy is also available. Please use department letterhead when requesting free books.

Author appearances, virtual or in-person, can often be arranged for book groups, classroom visits, symposia, book fairs, or other educational, literary, or book events.

Visit wtawpress.org for more information.

WTAW Press
PO Box 2825
Santa Rosa, CA 95405
wtaw@wtawpress.org

Other titles available in print and ebook from WTAW Press

Promiscuous Ruins by Julian Mithra

Eggs in Purgatory by Genanne Walsh

Mississippi River Museum Keith Pilapil Lesmeister

One Kind Favor: A Novel by Kevin McIlvoy

The Groundhog Forever: A Novel by Henry Hoke

Like Water and Other Stories by Olga Zilberbourg

Chimerica: A Novel by Anita Felicelli

Hungry Ghost Theater: A Novel by Sarah Stone

Unnatural Habitats and Other Stories by Angela Mitchell

And There Was Evening and There Was Morning: A Memoir by Mike Smith

The Truth About Me: Stories by Louise Marburg

Printed in the USA
CPSIA information can be obtained
at www.ICGtesting.com
JSHW021213150923
48203JS00004B/127

9 781733 661973